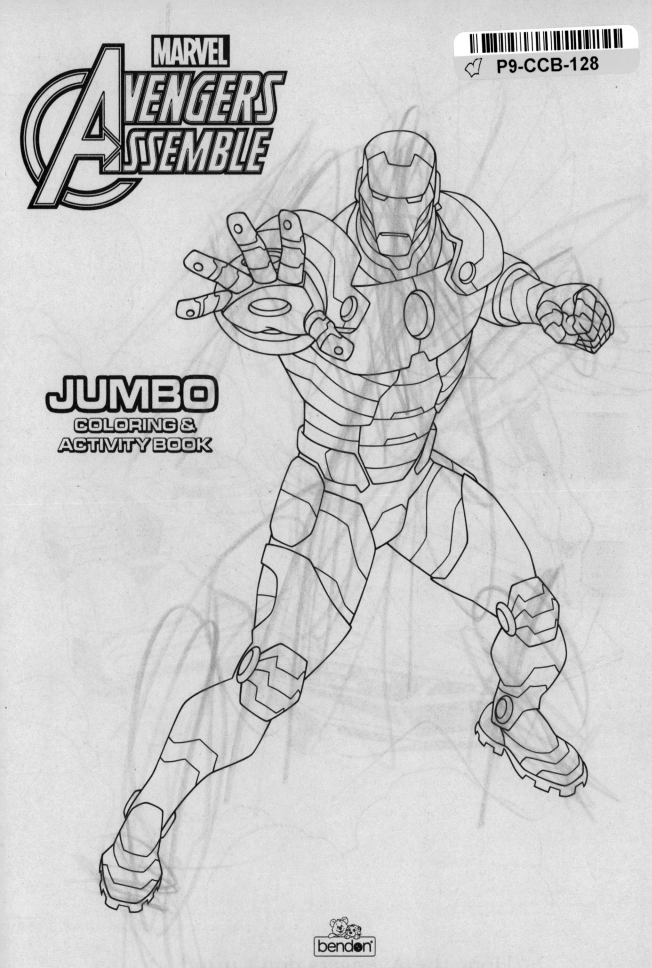

"Hope the Avengers don't mind…"

"…that I'm a little late."

The Avengers work with Nick Fury and his government agency S.H.I.E.L.D.
Can you fill in the blank to discover what S.H.I.E.L.D. stands for?

Strategic Homeland Intervention, Enforcement, and _____ Division

A. Laser-Fighting   B. Logistics
C. Label-Making   D. Logic-Enhanced

Answer: B - Logistics

"You've all been given your locations, Avengers.
Pair up and head out."

The Falcon has a question for Nick Fury. Cross out the first letter of the clue below and then every other letter to find out what it is.

IWOHBAATE ITSE TOHAE DEOMIERRAGIECNACNY?

Answer: What is the emergency?

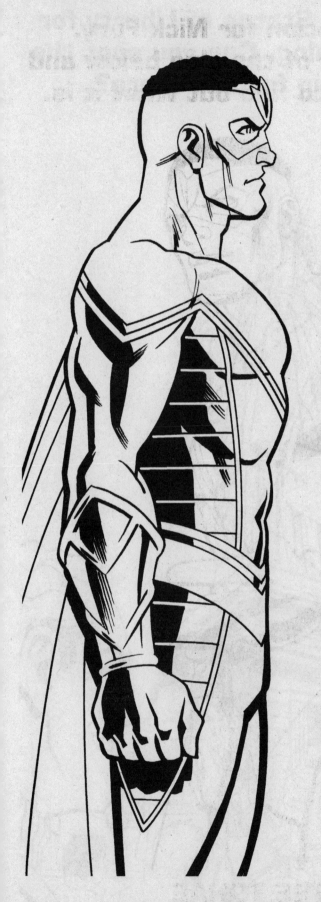

"No emergency. It's your training day."

The Falcon heads to the Statue of Liberty for the first part of his training. Can you spot the two Avengers waiting for him there?

Challenge # 1: flying lessons!

The Falcon is trying to catch up to Thor. Which path should he take to follow him?

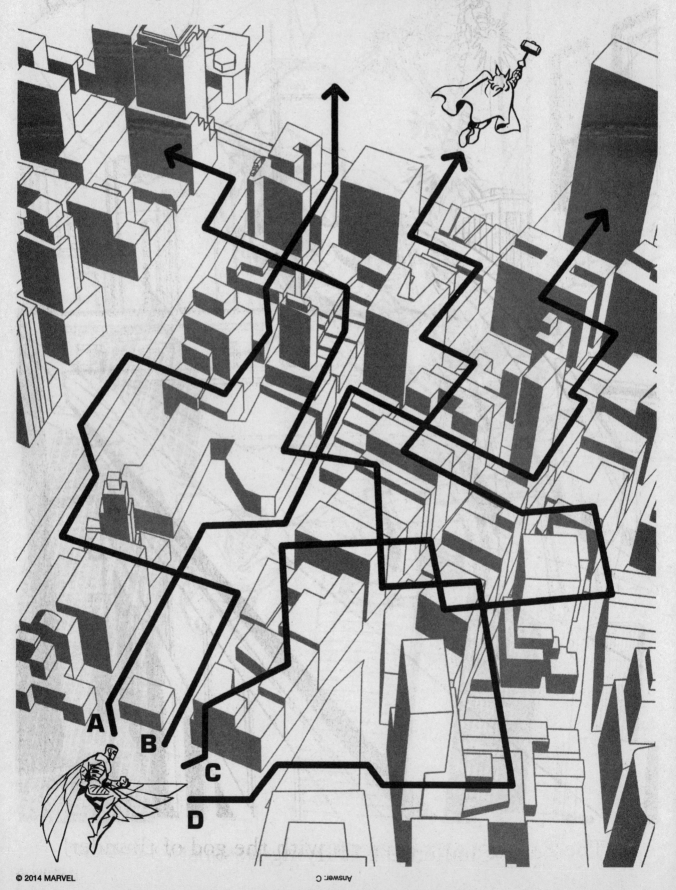

A

B

C

D

The Falcon can't keep up with the god of thunder!

Which one of these weapons is Thor's favorite?

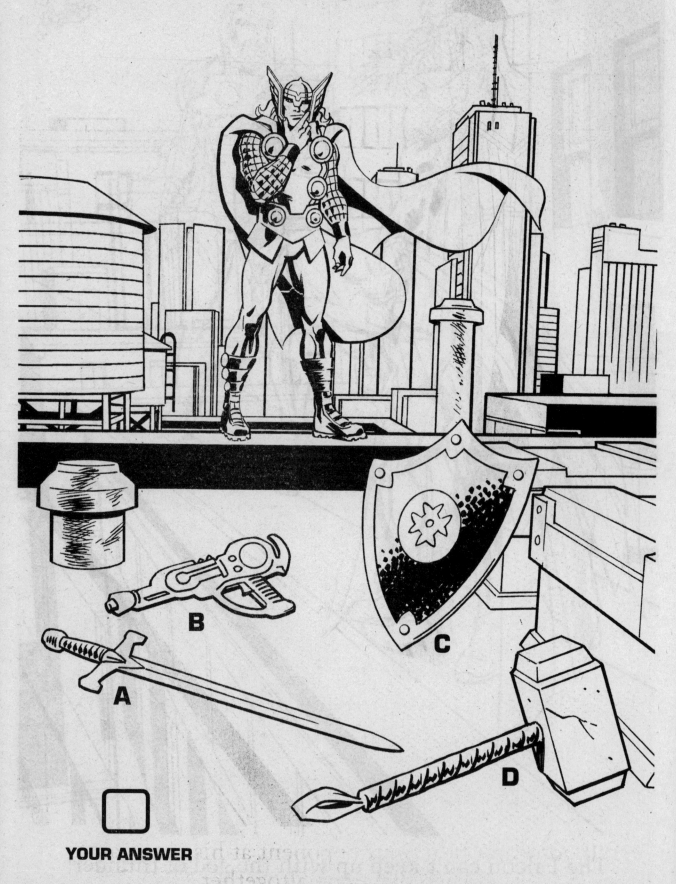

B

C

A

D

YOUR ANSWER

Answer: D

"If you can't beat your opponent at his own game,
change the game altogether."

Which of these powers does Iron Man's armor NOT have?

A. REPULSOR BLASTS

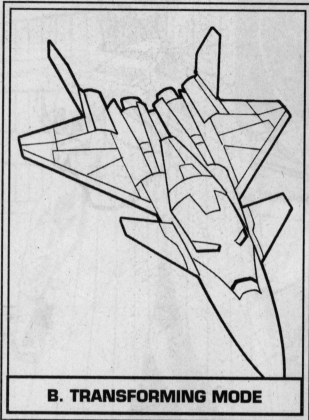

B. TRANSFORMING MODE

C. ARMORED SHELL

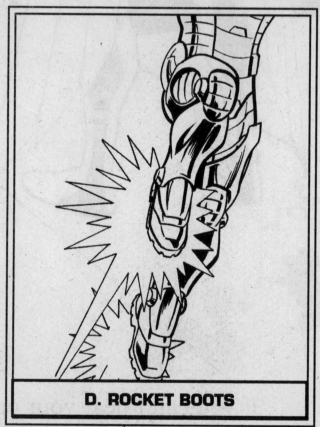

D. ROCKET BOOTS

Answer: B, Transforming Mode

A race through the woods!

Iron Man is just too fast!

What is Iron Man's secret identity? Unscramble the letters below to find out!

NYOT TRASK

Time to change the game!

Falcon's hard-light feathers explode on impact!

Challenge complete!

The Falcon's next test is in Brooklyn. Help him choose the correct route there on the map.

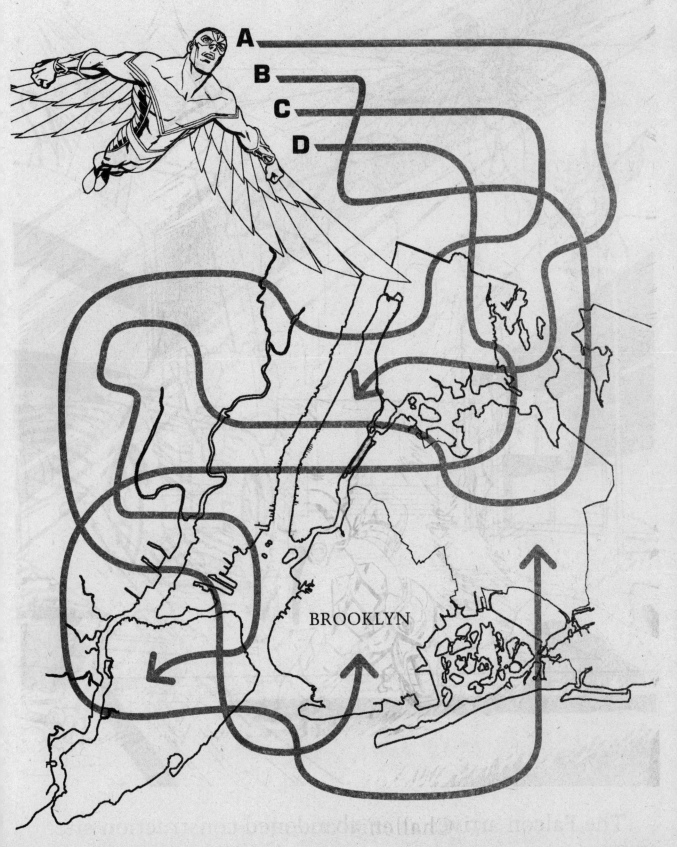

A
B
C
D

BROOKLYN

The Falcon arrives at an abandoned construction site.

A familiar attack!

Which shield matches Captain America's exactly?

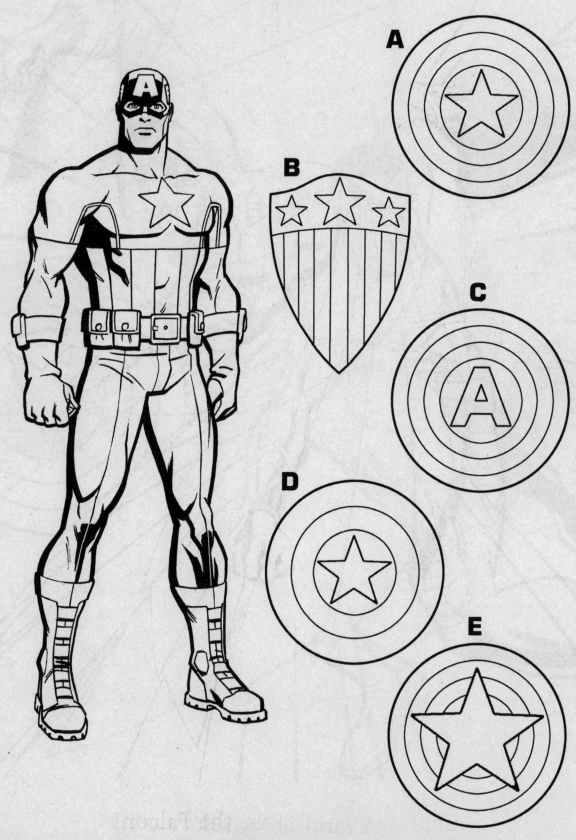

A

B

C

D

E

Answer: A

Captain America vs. the Falcon!

Captain America was just trying to get the Falcon's attention. Connect the dots to see the Falcon's real sparring partner.

Draw the missing comic panel.

Escaping to higher ground!

"If you can't beat your opponent with brute force,
look to your other strengths."

Help Hulk catch up to the escaping Falcon!

The Falcon is cornered!

Or maybe not!

Help the Hulk choose the right rope to use to climb out of the wet cement.

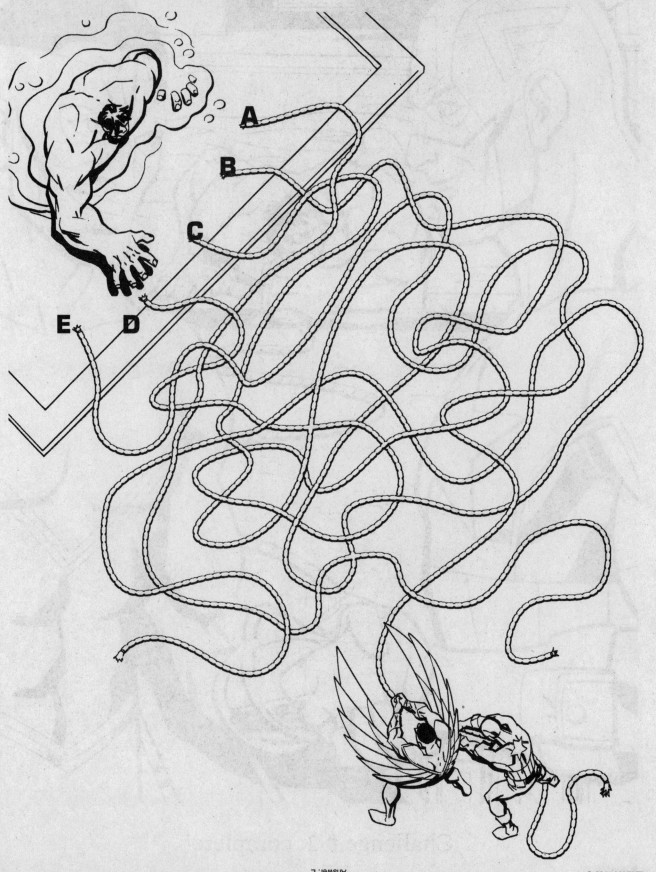

Challenge # 2: complete!

How many words can you make using the letters in:
THE AVENGERS

_____   _____

_____   _____

_____   _____

_____   _____

_____   _____

_____   _____

_____   _____

_____   _____

Possible Answers: save, have, teen, hear, here, see, gave, has, ate, gate, get, set, rest, vest, are, anger, nest, hare, stare, than

Match each hero to his or her symbol.

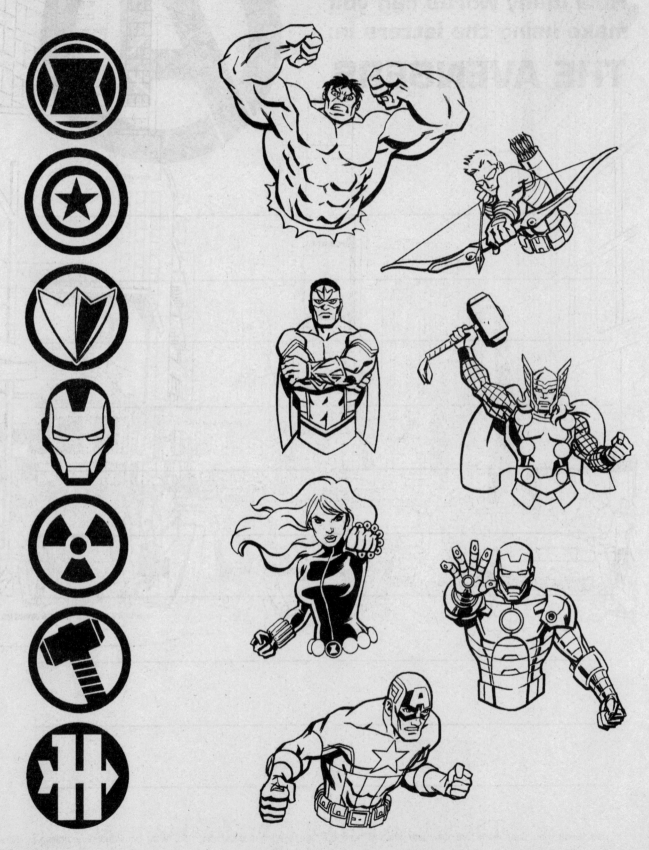

The Falcon arrives at his final test.

Find five things that are different on this page than on the last page. Circle them.

Answers: Hair missing from man on screen, car missing, 5 on building, man added on left, man missing hat on left.

"Black Widow's hiding somewhere in Times Square.
All you have to do is find her and bring her in."

Challenge accepted!

Spot Black Widow on the street below.

"No luck?"

"You just have to remember to take your time.
Look for the person who doesn't want to be spotted."

Draw the other half of the Falcon!

A Black Widow is no match...

for a bird of prey!

Draw the missing comic panel.

"Mission accomplished.
Head back to S.H.I.E.L.D. and report in."

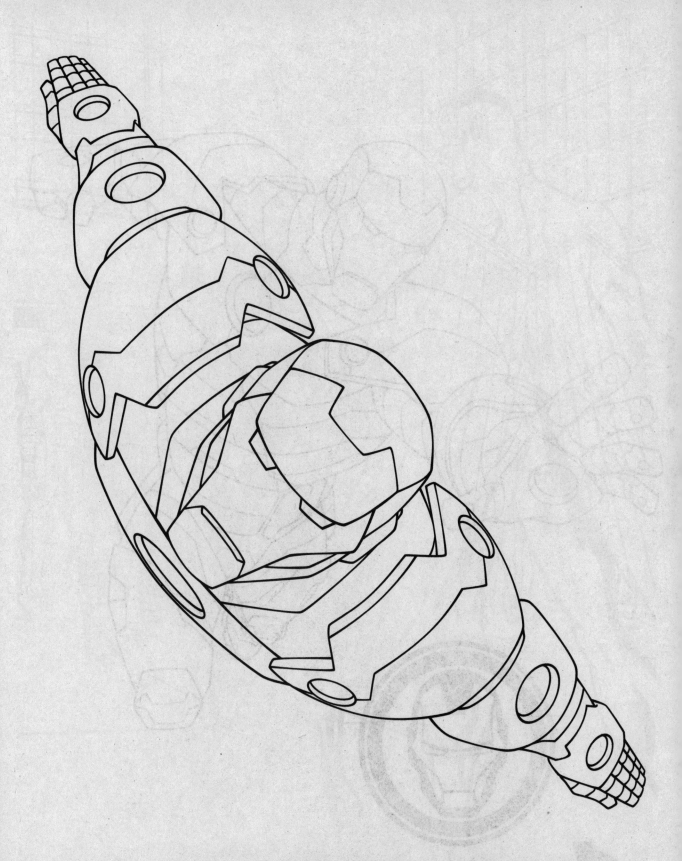

Armor up!

INVINCIBLE

The Big Guy

INCREDIBLE

Sentinel of Liberty

SUPER SOLDIER

Son of Odin

The Avenging Archer

SHARPSHOOTER

Widow's Bite

SUPER SPY

The Winged Avenger

THE FALCON

NICK FURY

Avengers assemble!